Bench by the Pond

A Poetry Gallery

Donna Harlan

BENCH BY THE POND
A POETRY GALLERY

iUniverse books may be ordered through booksellers or by contacting:

iUniverse
1663 Liberty Drive
Bloomington, IN 47403
www.iuniverse.com
1-800-Authors (1-800-288-4677)

Because of the dynamic nature of the Internet, any web addresses or links contained in this book may have changed since publication and may no longer be valid. The views expressed in this work are solely those of the author and do not necessarily reflect the views of the publisher, and the publisher hereby disclaims any responsibility for them.

Any people depicted in stock imagery provided by Getty Images are models, and such images are being used for illustrative purposes only. Certain stock imagery © Getty Images.

ISBN: 978-1-5320-8997-8 (sc)
ISBN: 978-1-5320-8998-5 (e)

Library of Congress Control Number: 2019919333

Print information available on the last page.

iUniverse rev. date: 11/27/2019

Contents

Preface and Acknowledgments ix

Communion

    Bench by the Pond..1

    Wood Floors...2

    Change 4

    January 6, 2018...6

    I Will Not Forget 7

    Christmas Photograph...................................8

    The Box...10

    Katie Crowing...12

    Dousing Dahlias..13

    Never Tire of You......................................14

    We 15

    Silver Spoon 16

    Blue 17

Whisperings

    More..21

    Hobson's Choice.......................................22

    Hoping for a Tiny Threat 23

    Crumbs in the Bottom of the Bag 24

    Red Cans 25

    Sauntering...26

    Wishing..27

    Breaking the Rules....................................28

    Eggs...29

    Levity 30

    Off-Kilter..31

    Rhyme..32

Seasons

Sweet William by the Gate 35

December Air...36

Ordinary Day 37

Quiet...38

Rotation..39

Beauty 40

Dawn..41

Waning Season...42

Spiderweb..43

Hope 45

Snowfall 46

Living

What Chore?...49

Peanut Butter and Passion Sandwich 50

Tokens 51

Trolls 52

Handbells 54

Muscle Memory 55

Another Birthday Candle 56

Sheet Music 57

Heirlooms

Magic Carpet..61

Floodplains..62

Present..63

Cursive Ys 64

Basement Shelves..65

Movie Night 66

Sixth Grade 67

Revelation
If I Am Deceived..71

Sleep..72

Praying..73

Worship 74

Heaven's Gate..75

Preface and Acknowledgments

Much is being required of me because much has been given. I've had over six decades to try to figure out what that "much" looks like and how to gift it to the world. I've tried to be logical and practical about making the most tangible differences through mentoring programs, volunteering at a hospital, delivering meals to the elderly, working with a homeless program, teaching adults to read, and teaching English as a second language. Of course, I enjoyed many of these moments and pray that there was good in them for others as well as myself. While these actions were from my heart, they were also distractions at times from hearing other callings that I deemed less important. Since that time of giving in a way that left me restless and frustrated at times, I have come to believe that the economics of blessing others cannot be measured in logical ways. So much of what pours forth from the soul leaves positive, lasting effects on the world.

This collection is a gift from my heart that was never a chore. These words have chosen me rather than my choosing them. You have the luxury of opening this gift away from my presence, so your reactions will be authentic. At the very least, I pray that you come away with gratitude for whatever "much" you have been given and a desire to gift the world with your true callings.

None of these words would be on a page without the strong, healthy relationships that I have enjoyed with my birth family, my husband and his family, and our children and their families. My husband, Jim, and our daughters, Katherine and Rebecca, have contributed encouragement as well as practical, technical help in the completion of this book. I am forever grateful for them.

Communion

Bench by the Pond

Come sit with me and watch the daisies grow,
the sun pulling them closer to the sky,
and we'll talk about the why
of that
and why fish jump,
not to mention the how—
no running starts on sinewy legs,
and do they hold their breath
leaving water for air?
I can't imagine
all the unasked questions
still unthought,
unsought.
Do turtles have opinions?
Who has the most dominion in the pond?
How many shades of green are in a frond?
Now look at how the daisies grew
as we sat together,
just we two.

Wood Floors

You said, "I like to hear wood floors creak,"
which I probably already knew,
but when you said it,
it became real,
and I was connected to you,
like we were the only two people
who've ever liked that sound since time began.
All of my wood floor memories flooded my mind at once,
the way water flooded our last house from a ceiling leak.
The memories came as a collage,
which I had to disassemble picture by picture.
My growing-up years and the old school,
whose wood floors seemed to breathe
in rhythm with my steps,
and the corresponding sweet, musty smell
that seemed comfortable and unforgettably endearing.
My first dorm room,
enormous by most standards,
whose floors had witnessed decades of drama,
not excluding my own.
My parents' house, whose floors talked all through the night,
the stuff of wild imaginings,
rivaled only by summer downpours on the tin roof.
Your parents' house of over fifty years,
whose carpet betrayed the perfect oak beneath.
Our last home that nearly daily let the sunshine rainbows
dance on the floor,
having bypassed the door in favor of the beveled glass.
Our sweet black cat, Molasses, playing with the light and colors.

The house we live in now, whose floors already have new stories,
having met family the other floors didn't know.
The way two-year old Maggie stood at the edge of the wood
and refused to walk on the shiny marble tiles as if she would drown.
I like to hear wood floors creak too.

Change

We read *The Good Earth* in the second-floor flat,
a book I presumed too mature for your fourteen years,
but it wasn't my choice,
just an assignment.
You grew up in that space,
home base when darkness fell every day at the same hour.
How could I have known that things were changing
when every day was repetitive?
We ate Singapore fried rice
and munched on fresh, damp saltines.
We took off our shoes at the door,
welcoming the shock of the cold marble floor.
You learned about iced coffee,
dances with boys,
the freedom of wandering in safe places.
Twenty years later and ten thousand miles took me back
to the coordinates of that once-welcoming complex,
the taxi stopping on cue,
but the driver confused about my dismay.
It was gone.
I cried.
I wanted to come back as much as I wanted to leave then.
I wanted to see the palm trees and walk around the pool,
but the glass and steel complex I saw was sterile and cold,
colder than any marble floor.
Too cold for the rush of heat on my face.
How dare anyone destroy that physical memory.
You grew up there.
I walked to the coffee shop you frequented,
overly aware of young moms with children

obviously on missions of meeting friends,
finding presents for parties,
getting to ballet,
or just being in a hurry because it felt normal.
The clock rolled back two hundred thousand hours,
and I saw myself in every one of the moms.
I cried in my coffee.
All around I heard laughter,
life,
movement.
Eight tissues later, I bought a beautiful dress for your daughter.

January 6, 2018

I don't know if you chose wisely
or if providence showed up,
but I rejoice in this reality,
celebrate this fulfillment of destiny,
revere the histories it represents
and carries forward.

I turn this page with anticipation,
trusting the author of this story,
having applauded insignificant events
now defined as markers in light of hindsight.

Treasured lives in this circle have linked hearts
in honor of your devotion to each other.
The future unfolds before us,
and we dare not blink for fear of losing a moment.

I bookmark this leaf
even as it's turned.
I will come back to this day,
reread this chapter,
memorize its moments,
and steal joy from this imprinted page.

I Will Not Forget

I laughed inwardly
when you first asked me
not to play with your dollhouse
while you were away.
You're six, and I'm sixty.
Laughter lingered,
slowly melting into sheer delight
that you believed I might.
You must have seen my joy
as I walked the plastic boy up the stairs,
our thoughts united in deep purpose,
my pretense convincing
even to an expert.
I crossed a barrier unseen
and entered into a moment of timelessness.
Reality keeled over,
like the rose-colored chimney
you bumped into,
and the farthest reaches of invention stepped in.
Your compliment,
phrased as command,
unseats all past praises.
No need to say, "Remember!"
I will not forget.

Christmas Photograph

The 1939 Firestone wall calendar
tells me that my father was ten
when the new bike was gifted to him.
The bike would have been his escape
after gathering eggs and milking cows.
Warping time,
it would diminish the half hour walk to school.
The wind in his face would power his freedom.
The image frozen in black and white
now becomes the vehicle that transports me
to a time before his life was colored with responsibilities
weighty and untimely.
Pure pleasure in those days of not knowing—
before the deaths of his brother,
his father,
his mother,

his first wife (my mother),
his sister,
his second wife,
before Parkinson's robbed him of agility
and rusted his gait.
He is ten and ready to ride.

The Box

I remember the way
you studied the wooden box
your dad sent from Afghanistan.
You were only three
and don't remember now.
You touched it softly over and over,
affectionate caresses
mingled with a quest for understanding
as if you were reading braille
in the deep carvings.
You played with my heart
the same way
without ever knowing it.
The way you practiced closing and opening
the drawer and lid

was tender and poignant,
without any drama,
which in some ways is harder to bear
than the classic maelstrom
of a three-year-old.
He came home,
and the box is mostly forgotten,
nearly abandoned,
which is how it should be.
No need now.
But the image remains
tucked away forever.

Katie Crowing

My grown-up self wants to apologize to our neighbors
for the six o'clock crowing!
Not by roosters
but by two-year-old you,
who simply had to run outside to wake the world.
Time has no meaning to you.
You let joy choose you this morning.
You abandoned yourself to your calling.
I feel the call too
and want to join your cock-a-doodle-doo
in harmony or even discord
loudly
and with zest and fervor!
Regrettably,
I know the time
and cannot crow aloud.
But, oh, my heart can sing!

Dousing Dahlias

I would not have watered the plants today,
especially with the chance of rain
and the cooler nights,
but I've seen the way you drag
this hose
and lift
this can
with the same conviction
that you apply to rescuing
the clean floor from a solitary
crumb.
Your inner voice denies you any choice.
Not so with me,
so I pretend to own your passion.
I've learned your ways during our fifteen thousand days
together.
Our differences are glue,
like poles of north and south.
No fear of identity loss
as I turn the faucet off
halfway through the task,
which you would never do,
to find paper and pencil
to record these thoughts
before I begin again
and stop again
to begin again.
I will douse the dahlias,
but I will not douse your dreams.

Never Tire of You

You can sneak up on people
but not on frozen peas in the grocery store,
which I find equally as delightful,
as if I were Crocodile Dundee.
Even friends may occasionally misplace my name in their
mental files,
but Amazon will never forget,
which is amusing in an offhand way,
not to mention their constant awareness of my every need.
The newspaper always begins with, "Good morning,"
before it proceeds to other things heinous
and says goodbye with strips of comics,
a lovely sandwich method
that unthinking humans might want to consider.
Traffic lights plead with us to be polite,
sometimes with the success of a substitute teacher before
holiday break.
But they stay the course without emotion,
setting a lovely example for all of us.
The greeting cards at the drugstore elicit more genuine laughter
than I've been privy to at cocktail parties.
But God forbid that those I love become predictable.
I adore the way my friends begin a conversation without context
clues,
anticipating my complete, but often missing, comprehension.
If you forget my name, I'll likely return the favor at a future
time.
My need for certainty is easily met by technology and sunrise.
I will never tire of you.

We

I choose to be
where I wouldn't be
if I were only me,
but I am half of we.
I choose not the place
but your movements
in my peripheral vision.
I choose not the doing
but the subtle familiar smell
of the essence of you.
I choose the whispered hush
of your breathing,
the awareness of your presence
in the room before I see or hear you,
knowing you choose
my laughter,
my tears,
and everything in between,
storing up
for lonely days
when breathing
will seem unworthy of effort
and place won't matter.

Silver Spoon

The wrong things grieve me at times.
The silver baby spoon
destroyed by the garbage disposal
was one I used as a child
then my children
and grandchildren.
Its patina was stunning.
Now it's gnarled beyond repair,
sitting in full view on the counter,
reminding me of my carelessness.
My great-grandchildren will eat applesauce
with a different spoon
and know nothing of what they missed,
which,
practically speaking,
is nothing.
They will grow up happy and strong,
Lord willing.
What about the spoon?
I don't really know,
but I loved it the way you love objects,
not the way you love grandchildren.
I will be careful with them
and pray they will always shine.

Blue

You cried when you unwrapped the cream pitcher
so carefully packed in Greece.
It was broken somewhere along the way.
Such a treasure—
the color of the Aegean Sea.
It was for my collection.
Your father pieced it together
slowly,
meticulously.
Only a solitary sliver was missing.
Now it has a front
and a back
and sits proudly in its place of honor.
The imperfection keeps the story alive
and will after we're gone.
The scar bears witness
of your tender heart
and makes me smile.

Whisperings

More

Yes, I was selfish coming here.
The empty space fills my spirit.
Storm and sun,
light and shadow
generously offer opposing views of beauty.
I feast on the sixty-three geese,
horizon hued with mulberry wine,
now streaked with a long, perfect V.
There was a time when I would have apologized
for being so ravenous,
so indulgent,
perhaps hearing words between lines,
judgments outside of earshot,
but no longer.
Decaying leaves resurrect my heart,
their bouquet redolent as myrrh.
The lake's brilliant glass
doubles expanse of sky
and my heart.
I am both still
and marauding.
My satisfied senses still yearning for more.

Hobson's Choice

Today I woke up to comfort,
safety,
provisions,
relationships,
beauty,
predictability,
possibility,
plans,
breathing space,
time gaps,
freedom.

Like cash I have to spend today,
no savings,
no interest earnings,
manna from heaven
today or today.
My Hobson's choice.

My only pressure, that of being mindful,
aware,
alive,
awake.

My only prayer,
one of gratitude
and all the above for everyone else.

Hoping for a Tiny Threat

Sometimes my life feels as still
as the warm September air,
frozen in the moment,
begging for the slightest drama
of wind
or passing nimbus,
hoping for a tiny threat
to prove perfection
isn't dull.
I need some yang to go with my yin,
some treadmill beneath my feet
to keep me moving,
even if aging is not my goal.
I want a video,
not a snapshot.
Tomorrow I will long for yesterday,
but today I need to know the world is turning.

Crumbs in the Bottom of the Bag

Much of my time is "wasted,"
like crumbs in the bottom of the chip bag,
which,
by the way,
I deem sacrificial
for the greater good of the bigger, more desirable chips.
"Make the most of every moment,"
has no meaning unless the lesser moments
are pronounced necessary,
or unless they aren't considered moments at all.
The paint left in the can has its role.
It is the keeper of the foyer wall history.
Try carrying a wall to Benjamin Moore.
Life is a whole,
not snippets of unexplained grandeur.
Those ten thousand hours were never wasted
in pursuit of arrival at "fill in the blank,"
even if you stopped at 9,999.

Red Cans

It's Friday.
Red cans line the streets,
along with recycle bin sidekicks,
doing the drill like a marching band.
Not one out of line,
as if proud of their community service.
Their cheery exteriors display a pleasant front,
doing more than justice
to the diapers and leftovers inside.
A picture of teamwork
and evidence of blessing.
No fires needed
to destroy yesterday's newspapers.
The cans contain more than garbage.
They spill over with a sure hope
of starting fresh tomorrow.

Sauntering

Sauntering is my favorite pace.
Indeed, I wish there was a race
for those of us with similar gait
and prizes if you show up late.
What is all the cheering for
when you are first outside the door?
You miss the trophy of the view,
and even if your ribbon's blue,
your blistered feet are screaming, "Ouch!
Please take me back, beloved couch!"
If I choose to float along,
my shuffle might create a song.
My steps will graduate to lilt;
I'll wonder how the trees were built
from little acorns dropped to earth
and know how much fresh air is worth.
I'll see the many shades of gold
and wonder how the sky can hold
the clouds so high and us below.
I wonder if I want to know
or simply love to saunter.

Wishing

Tomorrow is a special day.
I wish tomorrow was today.
But when tomorrow's said and done,
I'll want to see a full rerun.
Then I will say that yesterday
was such a time of great hooray,
and I will want a time machine
to see the things already seen.
But then I'll miss the here and now
and wish that time could just allow
the moments good and not the bad,
the ones that seem to make me sad.
If that were true, I greatly fear
that even if I had no tears,
I'd still be wishing for more flavor
in my life and things to savor.
So I must come to terms with this:
There's more to life than simple bliss.
I need the salty with the sweet.
Sometimes I need to eat a beet,
so when I eat my chocolate pie,
the difference is a longer sigh.

Breaking the Rules

I want to ask Michelangelo
if art should be at eye-level
or if craning your neck is worth the trouble.

I want to ask Monet how he knew
that details don't always matter
but light does.

I want to interview those who missed flight 175
on September 11, 2001,
how they feel about being late.

To Catherine Parr
I pose,
"How complicated is love?"

And to the clouds,
"Is it dark on the upper side?"

There must be rules for breaking the rules.

Eggs

Bob's gone now,
but I'll always remember how,
as he whisked dozens of eggs
in the huge aluminum bowl
for the teenagers at camp,
he said he hated eggs and wouldn't eat them.
I began firing questions of disbelief:
"What about their magic emulsifying properties
or all the many ways they can be cooked?
What about their ability to bind?"
How could he state such heresy?
Then, as quickly as I was taken aback,
I was taken back
to the time I shared his sentiments
and wished he could have sat at my childhood table
and seen my mother crumble crackers
into my slimy eggs and transform them into something edible.
Time and experience
have crumbled my need for the cracker bridge.
My mother would be proud.
I wish I could have converted Bob.

Levity

When the air is seventy-four,
I truly wish for nothing more.
I feel I could evaporate,
disseminate,
or vaporize,
and disappear
before your eyes.
Nerve endings on my skin quit work.
They have no cause to twitch or jerk.
Becoming lazy, they take leave,
and all that's left to do is breathe,
which I enjoy immensely so
when there are no cold winds that blow.
My body,
lightened by the ease,
is lifted up by gentle breeze,
and you will see me in the sky,
but you won't have to wonder why.
You'll know when temps begin to fall
that I'll descend
to
earth
again.

Off-Kilter

Off-kilter
is the filter I prefer,
not formula,
or recipe,
or pattern,
living large like Saturn,
dancing without music
but not without the sound
of rhythm found
within my head,
or living small like atoms,
always moving unbeknown
to those around
who think they're watching
but can't see
that side of me.

Rhyme

My mother read Robert Louis Stevenson to me,
and I loved going up in a virtual swing
almost as much as a real one.
Beatrice Schenk de Regniers composed a lovely verse
about keeping a poem in your pocket,
but not many people know her name.
I had to look it up,
although I can quote the poem
and often do inside my head.
I love it more than dearly.
The name Mary O'Neil isn't nearly as familiar to me
as the name of her imaginary first-grade teacher,
Miss Norma Jean Pugh.
Most of the time I feel I was born too early,
probably because I am sixty-three
and would like to live a lot longer,
but sometimes I believe I was born too late.
I miss the beauty of rhyme
that sticks in your head like glue.
It's hard to be sad
when you, "Sing a song of seasons."
I took a poetry class and learned,
to my dismay,
that the days of writing in rhyme are essentially over.
I hope to see its revival,
but until then,
I won't worry about what rhymes with "dream."
I'll just continue to imagine that one day
someone
who can't remember my name
will treasure a word that I wrote.

Seasons

Sweet William by the Gate

Sweet William by the gate,
so unaware his future fate
of frost and freeze and frigid air,
and if he was, why would he care?
For as he wilts to earth and dies,
his seed will catch the wind and rise
to places known and far beyond
to brighten days for other friends.

So if he bows his head at last,
don't make a fuss about his past,
but treasure in your memory's eye
the beauty that did not belie
reality that is today.
Rejoice with me and pray,
releasing thanks to He who gives
and takes away
to give again
another day.

December Air

Morning air before it rains
hangs
heavy
with anticipation
and promise,
runs into
lungs,
mind,
and soul
before it
falls.
Its aroma seeps
into places words cannot reach
or even people,
delivering
silent,
holy
awe
breath
by
breath.

Ordinary Day

Clouds are loud today,
sunlight whispering behind them,
coaxing
without effect.
The day will be gray;
the sky's dimmer turned to exquisite meal setting,
so I will accept this gift as if it were a treat,
as all days are.
I will breathe the wafting aroma of cut fescue,
satisfying as the sweet scent of cinnamon scones.
I will enter the world as the greatest of hallways,
its ceiling unseeable,
its walls hypothetical,
its boundaries defined solely by my physicality.
Of what things should I converse
in this majestic place?
I dare not destroy the levity,
the festivity,
of this extraordinary,
ordinary day.
I must bring my finest self to this occasion,
blow off the dust of complacency,
and gather interactions like a fresh floral bouquet.
I will be pleased as dusk falls,
barely imperceptible,
and offer gratitude.

Quiet

So quiet a dropping pin
would sound like ten.
So still my head is filled
with how the earth can be turning.
Air so nearly there I am a naked soul.
Panorama of trees inviting me to walk
inside the art of a perfect day.
Content to live this moment without audience.
Indeed,
to hoard it with pleasure,
to record the occasional snapping
of twigs,
and wonder why the birds are silent today.
Are they in awe of the way the creek
breaks
the tender hush as its whitewater
falls
across rocks
into clear?
My eyes are searching,
but for nothing,
taking captive
the wild,
never to be released.

Rotation

Morning feels new,
like earth's little pirouette
was a rebirth,
like air was washed clean,
but no one bothered to dry the leaves and grass,
knowing their saturation would spill out freshness,
like laundry that's left to dry in the breeze.
Of course, the spin wasn't little,
but it happens every day.
Dismissal is easy.
What is little?
A seed?
Pollen?
Invisible oxygen?
No.
Just overlooked.
Sun's brightness renews my vision.
I am reborn even as I age.
I am saturated,
surrounded by life.
Rocks throb with the heartbeat of earth.
I synchronize my breathing
with
the
beat.
I will not let the stillness betray the spin.

Beauty

Petals fall and lie,
a different kind of beauty,
not completely over
but nearly so.
Winds, both fierce and gentle,
design mosaic patterns,
turn the kaleidoscope of color,
draw our gaze to the more dramatic allure,
looking down at their future fate
and watching as they are swept into invisibility.
Are they fearful of tomorrow?
Emerging bud
to abandoned style
and stigma,
their presence stuns
then turns
to dust.

Dawn

Sunlight speaks in streaks,
crescendo rising,
saturating gray earth with silent glory,
blanking out the fullness of the leftover moon,
the greater light overcoming the lesser.
Deafening hush reverberates,
announcing newness.
No,
I do not overstate the coming of the dawn.

Waning Season

Waning season,
like the evening orb
on its way to new,
refuses to reflect light,
silently being without answering,
waiting for interval's end,
fulfilling undefined purpose
until it returns to its previous sliver,
awaiting rebirth.

Spiderweb

You worked so hard last night,
rebuilding a replica of the web
I took down yesterday.
I did it with regret,
so you have doubled my guilt today.
It is a work of art
and mastery of a skill
unique to the artist.
Removing it is not a criticism or commentary
on your symmetry or design.
They are perfect and functional.
I know you need to eat.
I would love to show you where to build,
but the only way I have to speak to you
is to remove this incredibly intricate,

dew-sparkled,
stunningly perfect,
annoying
web.

Hope

Unfolding tulip petals
open memory's recesses,
carry me back in time and place
to unending fields of color
and low, gray skies,
reminding me of simplicity's wealth
and the gift of experience.
The planted bulb
has fulfilled its promise
and joins with others,
multiplying hope
and applauding the resurrection
of the buried.

Snowfall

Another snow has fallen,
another blanket laid
upon the hills and valleys.
The sky such lovely gray.

Too cold to venture out,
the windows take me there.
Sixty years and still it's new.
So quietly it blares.

The timbre of the silence
as it hums an unknown pitch
is joined by other voices.
The harmony is rich.

No news that every flake
falls unique in its design,
but what about the gentle tints
as they paint the central plain?

Is this year's shade much different
than fifteen years ago?
Is it paper white or winter dove,
or a hue you've never known?

This beauty stands alone,
utterance not enhancing,
but still I had to speak my heart
because I found it dancing.

Living

What Chore?

If you're making the bed or sweeping the floor,
thinking about it heightens the chore.
But if you want to revel and bask,
relax and enjoy what could be a task.
Think about new ice cream flavors,
crazy ways to set a table.
Make up games that you would play
if you were with your friends all day.
Choreograph a birthday dance;
imagine goldfish wearing pants;
describe the smell of stormy air;
count the seconds that you can stare.
Beware of what these thoughts can do,
especially what they'll lead you to,
or you will wonder why you're pleading,
"Do you think the yard needs weeding?"

Peanut Butter and Passion Sandwich

In my heart I paint sunsets, waterfalls, and the skin of babies.
I write long, mysterious novels with surprise endings.
I photograph previously unknown species in the farthest jungles,
create flaky pastries consumed before they cool.
Broadway has my number.
The list is endless,
including simple tasks as well—
delivering a perfect punch line,
keeping dust at bay,
an empty laundry basket.
These gifts are from the heart,
not born of jealously or pride.
I share them with you now,
hoping you can taste the love
in your peanut butter and passion sandwich.

Tokens

Dropping a silver token into the slot,
the entrance gate opens.
Children whoosh by in both directions,
hoping to reach their favorite animal.
If someone ascends the unicorn before you,
we will need more tokens.
If you reach the unicorn first,
we will need more tokens.
If sunlight lasts
and songs delight,
we will need more tokens.
Yes.
We will need more tokens.

Trolls

Things I'll learn to do this year
are now becoming very clear.
I will learn to do more play,
and I will play away the day,
unless my mom tells me to quit,
to sit awhile and eat a bit.
I will not want to quick obey,
but I will choose to not delay.
And if I'm good, she'll tell me so,
and that will make me want to grow.
My braveness will increase by bounds,
and I will learn to measure pounds,
so useful for my helping hand
in cooking something truly grand.
I will learn to eat more spinach,
and my lessons I will finish
without a single whine or sigh,
and all my grades will be so high.
I will learn to soccer long,
and my muscles will grow strong,
Gymnastics will be my big thing.
You will want to watch me swing,
balance, roll, and nearly fly.
You won't believe how hard I'll try.
The year of six will be the best
as I begin so many quests,
imagining things no one has ever
thought before because I'm clever.
I will tell the time of day
and know when it is time to lay

my head upon my little bed,
and dream so deeply in my head
of what will happen when the sun
gets up and lends me light for fun.
And every day will start and end
adventuresomely, if I will tend
to staying true to all my aims,
most of which are playing games.
Of course, there are some other goals.
I really want to study trolls.

Handbells

I grasp the handles on the bells
and lift them in anticipation
of the third beat of the second measure.
From there,
it's a glorious march,
a dance,
a saunter,
a race.
I ring,
hoping for precision
but fully aware
that I might ring a little too gently,
too forcefully,
too quickly.
I let myself relax
and listen to the bells beside me,
the bells further from me.
The range of pitch extends in both directions.
Notes become music.
Mistakes are erased
as quickly as the tempo.
Bells are damped and put to rest.
A collective silence of wonder
becomes a music all its own.

Muscle Memory

We sort of comprehend
how the brain will often tend
to memories large and small,
events we can recall,
but when it comes to muscle,
we do so seem to tussle
with practice making best,
when we prefer to rest.

Another Birthday Candle

Another birthday candle
drips
pink
wax
on your princess cake,
fusing the smell of wax
with sweet vanilla icing.
Like emulsion on a negative,
the aroma burns an image
in the darkroom of my brain.
Photographs will freeze the smiles
and bring mine back as well,
but I will need to find this aroma
in the scrapbook of memory,
along with the sounds of laughter
and wrapping paper
being torn.

Sheet Music

The sheet music waits patiently,
never cringing at the same mistakes,
never giving up on the hope
that one day my notes will match hers.
She never compromises, though,
insisting she is right.
I can almost hear her cheer
when repetition reaps reward,
when muscles remember
without any help from my brain.
I know she applauds
when the song is fluid and flowing,
when it rises and swells,
and I have acknowledged and honored
her requests for dynamics and timing.
I long for the day
that I am perfect, like her,
not predictably the same,
like a robot,
but able to enjoy the freedom
of the dance without the constraint
of effort.
It could happen.
She is willing to wait.

Heirlooms

Magic Carpet

On summer nights, when air was weighted
with dampness and the length of day,
we pulled the mat, slick and green,
from the back of the Chevy wagon
and placed it on a chosen spot
as flat as we could find.
The mat agreed to catch our falls
as tumbling limbs began to flail.
Laughter rose and darkness fell,
and we were not content to leave
until the fire of lightning bugs
brought silent rhythm to the skies.
The mat was friend and knew us well
from sleepy nights while parents drove
to distant lands of cousins and canyons
and colorful, clouded canopies overhead.
A mythical, magical carpet ride.
Its last adventure is forgotten
as most things are that slip away
and fade like summer into fall,
becoming intermittent fire
and silent rhythms in our hearts.

Floodplains

Today I feast on yesterday's fare of remembrances,
unsolicited except for the door to thought,
propped open by a mop.

Water fills the bucket, and my mind's floodplains fill
with my mother's scent, gone for over forty years now.
Then there is the treasured musty aroma of my childhood basement,
stocked with dirty potatoes from the garden.

My brain on holiday
visits cheese shops, museums, churches;
runs into friends, unaged by years;
touches old clothing, metal chairs with vinyl seats;
holds babies who now have babies of their own;
walks on worn linoleum, long ago ripped away.

I linger wherever I find myself
until I find myself somewhere else.
I fold the towels slowly,
tucking the edges in toward the middle
and hear the ping of a text.
I smile.
This will be a memory tomorrow.

Present

No one told me that if I miss the moment,
I'll miss it again, over and over,
like a snapshot torn from a scrapbook
or a roll of exposed Pentax

Was I supposed to know that days and decades
would blur and wash away,
their only relic a furrow on my brow?

How can I remember to remember even now,
when days are exquisitely ordinary,
remarkably uneventful,
full of possibility but leaving large margins on the page;
unused space,
perhaps enhancing the art of life,
but unusable after pages are turned.
I cannot read what wasn't written.

I walk on the sands of time,
bend down, and try to hold it all.
My hands too small,
too inadequate.
I let the grains rain back to earth.
No more grasping.
I notice the warmth of light on my furrowed brow.
I am here now,
even if I forget.

Cursive Ys

It struck me as bold
for a thirteen-year-old
to pen his cursive Ys
so long and lavish,
as interesting as his gait
and my perception of his future fate,
which would doubtlessly
include a Nobel Prize.
So every time I had the chance,
I met his glance
and locked eyes
in a way that was probably weird,
but I was also thirteen.
I unashamedly copied his Ys
and own them to this day.
They are beautiful and bold.
I can't remember his name.

Basement Shelves

The year she died,
the basement shelves sagged with the weight
of homegrown green beans in Mason jars.
She had borne witness to the click of every lid
as each one promised a winter of plenty
in a season of coming need
that garden's return wouldn't be able to feed.
Her gift on a "good day," the sound of snapping beans
and the pressure canner whistle,
bringing the farmhouse kitchen to life
and securely sealing the harvest and the hours.
Shorter days brought heavier shelves,
heavier hearts
and plates as full as life allows.

Movie Night

Before streaming or DVD,
movie night was reel to reel
with a silver screen in our living room.
Dusk settled first,
then aunts and uncles in folding chairs,
cousins on the floor.
We knew the actors more than well
and recognized ourselves
with heads buried in hands.
Favorite scenes were rewound,
replayed,
relived.
Superpowers were declared
for those who ran backwards,
dived out of pools,
and decreased in age.
Christmas presents were rewrapped,
and snow rose to the clouds
with the same levity that filled the room.
That room of people no longer exists,
cast for a fleeting moment,
but the archives of those remaining
bear proof of the joy that was framed.

Sixth Grade

We essentially skipped sixth grade,
replacing the study of civilizations
with the unstated theme of war's incivility.
He was killed in Vietnam—Mrs. Neal's only son.

He stayed with us the rest of the year.
His mother's ghost posted homework
in the top, right-hand corner of the chalkboard,
and then disappeared behind a barrage of wet tissues.

He became our teacher,
relying on the immature instincts of twelve-year-olds
to display respect in the presence of grief,
acquiescence replacing frivolous mischief.

Nine thousand miles from the appointed explosion,
gravity took down paper airplanes.
We sat in hushed silence
as thunder raged.

Revelation

If I Am Deceived

If I am deceived,
oh, wonderful deception.
If God is not there loving,
oh, joy in thinking he is.
If someone has misled me,
I offer thanks for release.
If I have misled others,
how grateful they must be for me,
having brought hope
that knows no bounds.
If I return only to dust,
never again knowing conscious thought,
then praise to the thought
that I would live forever.
If I am deceived,
then I pray deception for you
for no soul is more at peace than mine,
no heart more content or secure.
If I am deceived,
I am completely,
eternally deceived
and grateful for deception.

Sleep

Sweet shadow of death,
dear sleep,
wash over me
like wind
and blow away
the bad
and leave
the best.
Without your healing grace,
morning will not lend its joy.
You are needed now,
but
one day the shadow of sleep
will fade,
and true morning
awakens my newborn soul.

Praying

Praying that I never dread
the laying down of head,
knowing there will come a night
when breath within me will take flight
and not return.

Praying all the joy I've found
will follow me to higher ground,
when waters round me rise
and bury what might otherwise
have shaken my soul.

Praying all the peace I've known
that through the many years has grown,
bringing comfort in dark times,
always keeping thoughts aligned
will stay my heart.

Praying smiles that on my face have swept,
leaving lines permanently etched,
revealing warmth of days gone by
will bring a long and pleasant sigh
to you.

Praying you live free and long
and that your life is full of song,
both heard and sung to carry on,
knowing days are never gone
when they are fully lived.

Worship

Quiet reverence fills the room,
stillness of hearts more pervasive
than the rustles and murmurs of restless children.
Breathing in rhythm,
a silent song of bound souls
is heard loudly by our audience of one.
Music swells and fills the air
that we inhale,
becoming part of us.
We are wrapped in grace,
awash in worship's unspeakable depths.

Heaven's Gate

How can someone without breath be so alive?
His presence fills the room with a century of stories,
a plethora of anecdotes.
Three pews fill with progeny who wouldn't have existed
had he not returned from war.
The memories pour out
like the sun
through stained glass.
The traveling light builds a bridge from heaven
to the golden oak floor,
making it sacred.
I want to remove my shoes and bow at this conjunction,
more compelling than a best-selling novel
or bustling metropolis,
more serene than a mountain peak
or meadow stream.
The moment defies definition.
It is otherworldly and will not last.
That's why I record it here,
in the hopes
that one day my passing will create a portal to heaven's gate
for those who sit
and wait.

Printed in the United States
By Bookmasters